101 Apple Recipes

by: Carole Eberly

Cover and Illustrations by Fran Porter

Copyright 1978 by **eberly press**

ISBN-0-932296-02-5

Hi!

Just a few notes before you grab your apple peeler and pie pan.

--You'll notice the scarcity of vegetable recipes here. (I did include two so my mother wouldn't feel she utterly wasted her time on all those childhood lectures about such things.) However, I made up for it by including 16 pie recipes covering everything from the downright sinfully gooey to "Plain Old Apple Pie."

--Use cooking apples, my favorite is McIntosh, for all recipes unless they say differently.

--Most of all, have a great time with this book. I did.

Carole

A FEW APPLE DEFINITIONS I COULDN'T RESIST

Apple Cation -- What you fill out when interviewing for a job.
Apple Rition -- A ghost.
Apple Itionist -- A person opposed to slavery.
Apple Ene -- Eisenhower's city.
Apple Latia -- A geographical region in North America.
Apple Oosa -- A kind of horse.

A FEW APPLE FACTS TO DAZZLE YOUR FRIENDS WITH

--More than 7,500 varieties of apples are now being produced.
--Apples are not native to North America. The first trees were planted by the
  first European settlers.
--Johnny Appleseed's apples were pretty awful tasting because the good ones
  are grown from grafts, not seeds. (Sorry, Johnny.)
--Our stone age friends knew how to preserve apples by freezing and sun drying
  them.
--More than 150 million bushels of apples are sold in the U.S. annually.
--Rub an apple slice on a wart to make it disappear. (If you believe that,
  I've got some real estate I want to sell you.)
                              *

WHAT EQUALS WHAT

Use six-eight medium apples for a nine-inch pie.
Use two pounds of apples for three cups of applesauce.
Use one bushel of apples for 16-20 quarts of applesauce.
Two large, three medium or four small apples make a pound.
Two-thirds of a pound makes two cups sliced apples.

(Got all that?)

WHICH APPLES TO CHOOSE

Variety	Characteristics	Season	Uses
McIntosh	Deep red, sometimes striped with green. Slightly tart.	Sept.-Feb.	Eating, baking, pies, salads
Jonathan	Bright red, small to medium, sweet-tart flavor.	Sept.-Feb.	Eating, baking, pies, salads
Red Delicious	Bright red, conical shaped with five points on bottom. Sweet.	Sept.-April	Eating
Golden Delicious	Yellow, conical shaped with five points on bottom. Juicy, sweet.	Oct.-April	Eating
Northern Spy	Bright striped and mottled red on yellow. Large. Very juicy.	Oct.-March	Eating, baking excellent in pies
Baldwin	Red, mottled with bright red. Mildly tart. Juicy.	Nov.-April	Eating, cooking
Idared	Bright red, smooth. Juicy.	Oct.-June	Eating, baking, pies, salads
Rome Beauty	Bright red with yellow. Slightly tart. Round. Stores well by bushels.	Nov.-May	Baking, pies
Wealthy	Bright red splashes over green skin. Medium. Juicy.	Aug-Dec.	Eating, pies
Winesap	Deep red tinged with yellow. Very juicy. Slightly tart.	Jan.-May	Eating, pies

SNACKS

BREAKFAST

BREADS

BEVERAGES

APPLE QUICHE

1 9-inch unbaked pie shell	2 eggs
5 large apples	1 c. evaporated milk
1 c. cheddar cheese,	1/2 t. salt
shredded	Dash nutmeg

Peel, core and slice apples into thin pieces. Arrange in pie shell. Sprinkle with cheese. Mix eggs, milk, salt and nutmeg together in small bowl. Pour over cheese. Bake at 350 degrees for 60-70 minutes. Serve hot or cold. *(Everyone will think you really worked hard. Ha! Ha!)*

*

APPLE PIZZA

11-ounce pkg, pie crust mix	1/2 t. cinnamon
5 medium apples	1/4 c. butter
1/2 c. flour	1/2 c. chopped walnuts
1/2 c. brown sugar	

Make up dough for two-crust pie. Roll out all dough to one 14-inch round. Place on ungreased 12-inch pizza pan. Turn under edges and flute. Core and slice apples thin on pie shell. Stir remaining ingredients, except nuts, together until crumbly. Sprinkle walnuts over pie and bake at 450 degrees for 25 minutes. Serve with ice cream or cheddar cheese.

*

APPLE BUTTER & CHEDDAR WAFFLES

Frozen waffles	Cheddar cheese, shredded
Apple butter	

Toast waffles. Spread each with 1 1/2 T. apple butter and top with 1 T. cheddar cheese. Place in broiler until cheese melts.

*

APPLE & CHEESE SNACKS

Unpeeled apple rings   Chopped walnuts
Cream cheese

Spread rings with softened cream cheese. Sprinkle with walnuts.

*

DOUBLE APPLE SANDWICHES

Apple, grated   Pitted dates
Cream cheese   Chopped walnuts
                             Apple bread

Mix apple, cream cheese, dates and walnuts. Spread on slices of apple bread.

*

PEANUT BUTTER & APPLE SANDWICHES

Unpeeled apple rings   Peanut butter

Spread slices of bread with peanut butter. Layer on apple rings.

*

APPLE & CHEESE CANAPES

5 medium apples   1 5-oz. jar cheddar cheese spread
16 slices white bread   1 5-oz. jar olive-pimiento spread
6-oz. cream cheese   Lemon juice

Core apples and cut into 16 thin rings. Cut rounds out of bread same size as
apples. Spread rounds with cream cheese. Place an apple slice on each. Brush with
lemon juice. Mix cheese spread together and fill centers of apple slices with
spoonfuls of mixture.

*

MAPLE APPLE GRANOLA

3 c. oats	2 c. powdered milk
1 1/2 c. wheat germ	1/4 c. sesame seeds
1/2 c. bran	1/4 c. unsweetened coconut
1 c. dried apples	1/4 c. salad oil
1/2 c. chopped walnuts	1/4 c. melted butter
1/2 c. chopped almonds	1 1/2 c. maple syrup

Mix ingredients and bake at 225 degrees 1 1/2-2 hours, stirring occasionally. Makes 8 1/2 cups.

*

BIRCHERMUESLI

1 c. oats	2 lemons, juice and rind
1 c. chopped almonds	4 T. evaporated milk
2 c. yogurt	4 grated apples
1/2 c. orange juice	Brown sugar

Mix ingredients and sweeten to taste with brown sugar. Add one or more sliced fruits that are in season such as strawberries, bananas, peaches. Serves 4-6. *(Easier to make than pronounce.)*

*

APPLE FRITTERS

1 1/2 c. flour	3 eggs
1 T. sugar	2/3 c. milk
2 t. baking powder	2 T. salad oil
1/2 t. salt	3 c. diced apples

Sift dry ingredients. Beat eggs, milk and salad oil. Add dry ingredients and mix just until moistened. Stir in apples. Drop from tablespoon into hot (375 degrees) shortening. Fry till puffy and brown, 3-4 minutes, turning once. Drain on paper towels. Sprinkle with powdered sugar.

*

APPLE MUFFINS

2 c. flour
1/4 c. sugar
1 T. baking powder
1 t. salt
1 t. cinnamon

1 apple, diced
1/2 t. nutmeg
1 egg
3/4 c. milk
1/4 c. salad oil

Mix dry ingredients with apple. Beat wet ingredients and stir in dry ones, stirring just till moistened. Fill muffin papers 2/3 full. Bake at 400 degrees for 20-25 minutes. Makes 12.

*

APPLE CORNBREAD

1 c. cornmeal
1 c. flour
1/3 c. sugar
1 T. baking powder

1 t. salt
1 egg
1 c. milk
1/4 c. salad oil
1 apple, diced

Mix dry ingredients. Beat wet ingredients, stirring in dry ones. Add apple. Pour into well-greased 9-inch square pan. Bake at 425 degrees for 20-25 minutes.

*

APPLE PANCAKES

1 c. flour
1/2 t. salt
1 t. baking powder

1 egg
1 c. milk
1 T. salad oil
1 apple, diced

Mix dry ingredients. Beat wet ingredients and stir in dry ones. Mix in apple. Bake on hot greased griddle.

*

CRUNCY APPLE COFFEECAKE

1/4 c. flour
1/4 c. brown sugar
1/2 t. cinnamon
1/4 t. nutmeg
2 T. butter
1 3/4 c. flour
1/2 c. sugar

1 T. baking powder
1/2 t. salt
1/2 c. butter
3/4 c. milk
1 egg, slightly beaten
2 apples, peeled and sliced
   thin

Mix flour, brown sugar, cinnamon and nutmeg in small bowl. Cut in 2 T. butter until mixture is crumbly. Set aside. Combine flour, sugar, baking powder and salt in bowl. Cut in 1/2 c. butter. Add milk and egg, stirring just till moistened. Spread batter in greased 9-inch square pan. Arrange apple slices on top. Sprinkle with topping. Bake at 400 degrees for 30-35 minutes.

*

QUICK APPLE BREAD

1/2 c. shortening
1 c. sugar
1 1/2 T. sour milk
2 eggs
1 t. vanilla
1 t. baking soda
1 t. salt

2 c. flour
1 c. cider
1 1/2 c. apples, chopped
1/2 c. walnuts, chopped
2 t. sugar
1/2 t. cinnamon

Cream shortening and sugar. Add sour milk, eggs and vanilla, blending well. Alternate adding dry ingredients with cider. Stir in apples and walnuts. Pour into a greased loaf pan. Sprinkle with mixture of sugar and cinnamon. Bake at 350 degrees for 1 hour, 15 minutes.

*

APPLEJACK

Put hard cider outside to freeze in winter. Whatever doesn't freeze is applejack.

CIDER PUNCH

1 c. sugar	1 c. orange juice
1/4 c. lemon juice	2 1/2 c. ginger ale
2 1/2 c. cider	

Heat sugar and lemon juice in saucepan until sugar dissolves. Add to cider and orange juice. Chill. Add ginger ale before serving.

*

HOT MULLED CIDER

1 gallon cider	1 stick cinnamon, broken
1 c. brown sugar	2 t. whole cloves
1/2 c. butter	

Bring cider to a boil. Add remaining ingredients and simmer over low heat, stirring until sugar dissolves. *(The best!)*

*

CRANBERRY CIDER PUNCH

1 c. sugar	2 c. cranberry juice
1/2 c. water	1/4 c. lemon juice
1 quart cider	1 quart ginger ale

Boil sugar and water in saucepan. Add to the cider and juices. Chill. Before serving add the ginger ale.

*

COGNAC CIDER PUNCH

1 c. orange juice	1/4 c. maraschino cherry juice
1 c. lemon juice	2 quarts cider
1 c. pineapple juice	1 c. cognac

Mix all ingredients together and serve over a block of ice.

*

HOW MANY APPLE CLICHES CAN I GET INTO ONE PARAGRAPH?

"Why, he's as American as apple pie. He's the apple of my eye, even though he's rotten to the (apple) core. You know what they say, 'One bad apple spoils the barrel.' He's a bad apple for sure. He's an apple polisher and wants everything in apple pie order. When we took a trip to the Big Apple, he was always upsetting the apple cart. When I drank the water and came down with the green-apple-quick-step he kept saying, 'An apple a day keeps the doctor away.' Still, he believes in apple pie and mother-hood."

Phew! (I couldn't figure out where to put in Adam's apple.)

PRESERVES

JAMS

SAUCES

SALADS

FREEZING APPLE SLICES

Wash firm, mature apples. Peel, core and slice. Soak in a solution of 2 T. salt per gallon water for 15 minutes. Rinse and drain. Dry with paper towels. Cover all surfaces with sugar and pack in freezer containers.

For a frozen apple pie filling try this: Peel, core and slice 18 large apples. Put in a pot with 6 T. butter, 3 c. sugar, 3 t. cinnamon and 1 t. nutmeg. Cook over very low heat 15 minutes, stirring occasionally. Cool filling. Pour into three freezer containers. Enough for 3 9-inch pies. *(I would have made this a separate recipe, but then I'd have had to change the title of this book.)*

*

SUN DRIED APPLES

Wash firm, mature apples--preferably Northern Spys or Baldwins. Core and slice into rings. Brush well with a solution of 2,000 milligrams of ascorbic acid (Vitamin C tablets will work) to a quart of water. Place on a clean cloth and cover with a canopy of cheesecloth. Place in a spot that receives sun all day. Drying time depends on temperature, sun and humidity--which, ideally, should be low. Test fruit by tearing it apart. It should have a flexible "kid glove" texture. When done "pasteurize" it by putting it on baking sheets in a very low--175 degrees--oven. This will get rid of any little bad things that want to share your apple rings.

If you don't see the sun much where you live because of pollution, after coating the apple slices with ascorbic acid put them in the oven at a very low setting--not more than 175 degrees. Apple slices need air to circulate around them so put them on cake cooling racks on the oven racks to make a mesh screen. Keep the door ajar while baking. When they're through, 4 to 14 hours, process as above. Package in plastic bags.

*

BAKED APPLE SLICES

6 medium apples	1/3 c. brown sugar
1/4 c. water	1 t. cinnamon

Peel and core apples. Cut into rings and place in large saucepan. Pour on water, sprinkle with sugar and spices. Cover and simmer 20-30 minutes.

*

BATTER FRIED APPLE RINGS

1 c. flour	3/4 c. milk
1 1/2 t. baking powder	1 egg
2 T. sugar	4 large apples
1/2 t. salt	Sugar & cinnamon

Sift dry ingredients. Add milk and egg, beating well. Peel and core apples. Slice into 1/4-inch rings. Dip rings in batter and fry in 1/2-inch hot shortening until golden brown. Drain on paper towels. Sprinkle with sugar and cinnamon mixture.

*

FRIED APPLES

6 large apples	1/4 t. salt
4 T. bacon fat	1/4 c. water
1/2 c. sugar	

Core and slice apples into thick pieces. Heat bacon fat in frying pan and drop apple slices in. Cover and cook until brown. Add sugar, salt and water. Simmer until apples are tender.

*

FRIED GREEN APPLES

4 T. shortening	3/4 c. sugar
6 green apples	1/2 t. cinnamon

Heat shortening in frying pan. Core and slice apples. Drop into skillet with sugar and cinnamon. Cook slowly, stirring occasionally until apples are browned.

*

CURRIED APPLE SLICES

3 c. apple slices	1/4 c. sugar
1/4 c. melted butter	1 T. curry powder

Mix all ingredients together. Broil 10-12 minutes. Great with meats.

*

CINNAMON APPLE RINGS

1/4 c. sugar   1/2 c. red cinnamon candies
1 1/2 c. water   4 apples

Combine sugar, water and candies in frying pan, heating until candies melt. Core apples and slice into rings. Simmer in syrup until transparent.

*

SPICED CRAB APPLES

4 c. sugar   2 sticks cinnamon, broken
2 c. water   2 t. whole cloves
1 c. vinegar   1 1/2 qt. crab apples

Heat sugar, water, vinegar, cinnamon and cloves to boiling. Drop 1/6 of the apples into syrup and cook until tender. Pack in hot, sterile jar. Add hot syrup to 1/2-inch from top. Seal. Repeat with remaining apples. Makes 6 pints.

*

CRAB APPLE PRESERVES

1 lb. crab apples   1 c. water
1 lb. sugar   1/2 lemon, sliced thin

Peel crab apples. Boil sugar, water and lemon peel. Add crab apples and cook until tender. Remove from heat and let stand overnight. Pack fruit into jars, pouring syrup on top. Seal.

*

APPLE RELISH

6 c. chopped apples   1 t. mustard
2 green peppers, chopped   1/2 c. vinegar
1 c. onion, chopped   1 c. water
2 red peppers, chopped   1 1/2 c. sugar

Mix all ingredients together in pot. Cook slowly for 1/2 hour. Pack in hot, sterile jars and seal.

OLD FASHIONED APPLE BUTTER

5 lb. tart apples	3 t. cinnamon
3 c. apple cider	1 t. cloves
4 c. sugar	

Peel, quarter and core apples. Bring apples and cider to a boil in heavy saucepan. Reduce heat and simmer, covered, for 20-25 minutes. Puree apple mixture in a blender. Add sugar and spices, blending well. Pour puree into a shallow baking dish and bake at 300 degrees for 2 hours, or until thick enough to hold its shape. Pour into hot sterile jars and seal. Makes about 10 6-oz. jars.

*

APPLE JELLY

Apples	Sugar
Water	

Quarter and core apples. Simmer in saucepan, with just enough water to cover, until soft. Strain out juice. Add 1 c. sugar for each cup juice. Simmer until mixture reaches 220 degrees. Pour into hot, sterile jars and seal. Four cups juice makes about 4 6-oz. jars.

*

APPLE MARMALADE

6 lb. tart apples	3 lb. sugar
3 lemons	1/4 c. water
1 oz. fresh ginger root	

Core apples and slice into thin pieces. Cut peel from lemons into thin strips. Grate ginger. Put apples, peel, ginger, sugar and water into pot. Squeeze juice from lemons and bring to a boil. Cook at a low boil until syrup is thick. Stir often. Pour into hot, sterile jars and seal.

*

INSTANT APPLESAUCE

1/4 c. cider or water   1/4 c. sugar
4 medium apples   1/8 t. cinnamon

Peel, core and slice apples into thick pieces. Put cider or water and apples into blender. When smooth, add sugar and cinnamon. Blend until smooth. *(Good.)*

*

HONEY APPLESAUCE

12 medium apples   1/2 t. cinnamon
2 1/2 c. water   1/4 t. nutmeg
1/2 c. honey

Peel, core and slice apples into thick pieces. Cook with water in saucepan until soft. Press through food mill into another saucepan. Stir in honey and spices, simmering over low heat until fairly thick. *(Better.)*

*

CHUNKY APPLESAUCE

Peel, core and slice 6 apples into thick pices. Cook with just enough water or cider to keep from scorching in a covered saucepan. Stir occasionally. Mash up apple pieces a little. Sweeten to taste with brown sugar. Add a dash or two of cinnamon and nutmeg. *(Best.)*

*

SMOOTH APPLESAUCE

Follow the above recipe but grind apples through a food mill at the end of cooking. Add sugar and spices to taste.

*

(Liberate yourself from that yucky, canned stuff in the stores. Once you make your own applesauce, you'll never buy another can.)

WALDORF SALAD

2 c. diced apples	1/4 c. mayonnaise
1 c. diced celery	1/2 c. whipped cream
1/2 c. chopped walnuts	

Mix apples, celery and walnuts with mayonnaise and whipped cream.

*

APPLE SLAW

1 Spanish onion	1/4 c. dill pickle slices
2 apples	French dressing
4 c. shredded red cabbage	

Slice onion into rings. Core apples and slice thinly into rings. Combine onion, apple, cabbage and pickle. Moisten with French dressing.

*

GOLDEN DELICIOUS SALAD

1 6-oz. pkg. lemon gelatin	3/4 pint cottage cheese
1 1/2 c. boiling water	1/2 c. chopping nuts
2 c. orange juice	2 c. diced golden delicious apples

Dissolve gelatin in water. Add orange juice. Pour 1-inch layer in 2-qt. mold. Chill until firm. Chill remaining gelatin until syrupy. Add remaining ingredients and pour over firm gelatin. Chill until set.

*

RED APPLE SALAD

4 apples	3 c. water
1 1/2 c. sugar	1/2 c. cottage cheese
1/2 c. red cinnamon candies	1/4 c. chopped green pepper

Pare and core apples. Heat sugar, candies and water until candies dissolve. Cook apples slowly in covered pan in this syrup. Turn apples occasionally. Drain and chill. Stuff apples with cottage cheese and green pepper.

*

VEGETABLES

STUFFING

MAIN DISHES

BAVARIAN APPLE CABBAGE

1 medium apple 1/4 c. white wine
1 medium head red cabbage 2 T. vinegar
3 T. butter 1 t. sugar
1 bay leaf Salt & pepper

Peel, core and slice apple. Shred cabbage and add to butter with apples, mixing well. Cover and cook on low heat for 10 minutes. Add remaining ingredients. Cover and cook for 45 minutes, stirring occasionally. Serves 6.

*

SCALLOPED SWEET POTATOES & APPLES

3 medium sweet potatoes 1/2 c. apple cider
1/2 c. butter 1/2 t. mace
3/4 c. brown sugar 2 medium apples, pared and sliced

Boil potatoes in water for 25 minutes. Drain and let cool. Peel and cut into 1/4-inch slices. Melt butter in small pan. Add brown sugar, cider and mace. Bring to a boil, stirring until sugar dissolves. Simmer, uncovered, 10 minutes. In baking dish, layer potato and apple slices. Spoon half of syrup over potato mixture. Bake, covered, at 400 degrees for 25 minutes. Remove cover and bake 25 more minutes, basting with remaining syrup. Serves 6.

*

APPLE RAISIN STUFFING

1/2 c. minced onion 1 t. salt
2 c. diced apples 2 t. poultry seasoning
4 c. soft bread crumbs 1/2 c. melted butter
1/2 c. raisins

Combine all ingredients, mixing well. Makes enough to stuff 6-7 lb. capon or 8-10 lb. turkey.

*

SAUSAGE APPLE STUFFING

1/2 c. sausage	1 c. soft bread cubes
1/2 c. diced apples	Salt & pepper
2 T. chopped onion	Hot water

Fry sausage, apple and onion until cooked. Add bread cubes, salt and pepper to taste and enough hot water to make a good stuffing. Enough for a 2-3 lb. chicken.

*

APPLE STUFFING

2 T. butter	1/2 t. nutmeg
4 T. chopped onion	Salt & pepper
4 diced apples	2 T. parsley, chopped
4 c. bread cubes	Water
2 eggs	

Cook onions and apples in butter until tender. Add bread cubes, eggs, nutmeg, salt and pepper to taste and parsley. Mix well. Add enough water to make a good stuffing. Enough for a 6-8 lb. turkey.

*

APPLE STUFFED PORK CHOPS

6 pork chops, with pockets for stuffing	2 c. stuffing
	Cooking oil
	1/4 c. water

Put 1/3 c. stuffing (Apple, Sausage Apple or Raisin Apple) in pocket of each chop. Secure with wooden picks. Brown chops on both sides in oil. Add 1/4 c. water and simmer for 45-50 minutes, or until tender.

*

SHERRIED CHICKEN & APPLES

3 large apples	1 t. paprika
1 T. lemon juice	1 t. salt
1/4 c. sherry	1/4 t. pepper
1/4 c. brown sugar	1/4 c. salad oil
Flour	1/2 c. apple cider
1/2 c. butter	1/4 c. sherry
Sugar & cinnamon	2 c. light cream
1/2 c. flour, divided	1 frying chicken, cut up

Core apples and cut into sixths. Mix lemon juice, sherry and brown sugar. Pour over apple wedges and let stand 1 hour. Drain apples and dip in flour. Fry slowly in butter until golden and tender. Sprinkle with sugar and cinnamon. Serve with chicken. Combine 1/4 c. flour, paprika, salt and pepper. Coat chicken pieces. Brown in salad oil. Add cider, cover and simmer until tender, about 30-40 minutes. Add sherry. Cook 2 minutes. Remove chicken to platter. Add remaining flour to pan and mix with dripping. Add cream. Stir over low heat until smooth and thick. Spoon over chicken. Serves 4.

*

APPLE MEAT LOAF

2 1/2 lb. ground beef	1/4 c. minced onion
1 1/2 c. bread crumbs	2 T. mustard
2 c. diced apples	2 T. Worcesterhsire sauce
1 egg	1/3 c. catsup

Mix all ingredients thoroughly. Bake in a greased loaf pan at 350 degrees for 1 1/4 hours. Serves 6-8.

*

APPLESAUCE MEAT BALLS

Follow the Apple Meat Loaf recipes, substituting 1 1/2 c. applesauce for the diced apples. Shape into 2-inch balls and place in baking dish. Pour 1/3 c. catsup and 1/4 c. water over top and bake at 350 degrees for 45 minutes. Serves 6-8.

*

APPLE & HAM CASSEROLE

3 1/2 c. ground cooked ham	1/4 t. ground cloves
1 c. soft bread crumbs	1 T. minced onion
1 egg	3 apples
1/2 c. milk	1/3 c. brown sugar
1 T. mustard	2 T. butter

Mix together ham, bread, egg, milk, mustard, cloves and onion. Put in baking dish. Peel, core and slice apples. Arrange apples on ham mixture. Sprinkle with brown sugar and dot with butter. Bake at 375 degrees for 40 minutes. Serves 4-6.

*

BAKED APPLES & SAUSAGE

Apples   Sausage meat
Brown sugar

Core apples and peel 2-inch strip from tops. Sprinkle centers with brown sugar.
Stuff with sausage meat and bake at 350 degrees for 1 hour. *(How simple can you get?)*

*

APPLE PORK BALLS & SAUERKRAUT

1 egg   1/4 c. corn meal
1 lb. ground pork   2 T. butter
1/4 t. nutmeg   2 c. sauerkraut
Dash cinnamon   1 c. sour cream
1 medium apple

Beat egg. Mix in pork, nutmeg and cinnamon. Peel, core and grate apple. Mix
ingredients together and form into 2-inch balls. Roll in corn meal. Heat butter in
frying pan and add meat balls. Brown well. Reduce heat to low, cover and cook 30
minutes. Heat sauerkraut in saucepan. Mix sour cream in with pork balls. Heat, but
don't boil. Drain sauerkraut and place on serving dish. Spoon pork balls and sauce
over top. Serves 4.

*

MEAT & APPLE RING PATTIES

1 lb. ground pork   1 egg
1/2 lb. ground beef   1/2 t. salt
2 T. chopped onion   1 apple

Mix pork, beef, onion, egg and salt. Shape into 12 patties. Peel, core and cut
apple into 6 rings. Place 1 ring on each patty. Cover with another patty, pressing
to seal edges. Bake at 350 degrees 45 minutes.

*

DESSERTS

GOOEY THINGS

APPLE PANDOWDY

4 large apples	2 t. baking powder
1 c. brown sugar	2 T. sugar
1/2 t. cinnamon	1 t. salt
3 T. butter	6 T. butter
1 1/2 c. flour	2/3 c. milk

Peel, core and slice apples in bottom of greased 8x8-inch baking pan. Sprinkle with brown sugar and cinnamon. Dot with butter. Sift flour, baking powder, sugar and salt. Cut in butter. Add milk to make soft dough. Take out small pieces of dough and press between the palms of your hands. Lay on top of apples, pressing dough together to form one big piece. *(It sounds dumb, but it works.)* Bake at 350 degrees 45 minutes. Cut into squares and turn upside-down to serve. Serve with nutmeg-flavored cream. *(Super!)* Serves 6.

*

APPLESAUCE BROWNIES

1 1/4 c. sugar	1/2 t. cinnamon
1/2 c. butter	2 c. applesauce
2 c. flour	2 eggs
1 1/4 t. baking soda	1/2 c. chopped walnuts
2 oz. melted bitter chocolate	6-oz. pkg. chocolate chips

Beat sugar and butter together. Sift dry ingredients. Add to sugar and butter with chocolate, applesauce and eggs. Beat well. Pour into greased 9x13-inch pan. Sprinkle with walnut and chocolate chips. Bake at 350 degrees for 30 minutes. *(This is actually more of a cake than a brownie, but it is brown and I had to call it something.)*

*

APPLE BARS

1 c. flour	1/2 c. butter
1/2 t. salt	1 egg
1/2 t. baking soda	1 t. vanilla
1 t. cinnamon	1/4 c. chopped walnuts
1 1/2 c. uncooked oats	2 c. thinly sliced pared apples
2/3 c. brown sugar	Powdered sugar

Sift flour, salt, baking soda and cinnamon. Beat in oats, sugar, butter, egg and vanilla. Press half of dough in bottom of greased 9-inch square baking dish. Sprinkle walnuts over dough. Arrange apple slices over nuts. Roll remaining dough between waxed paper to form 9-inch square. Place dough over filling and press lightly around edges. Bake at 350 degrees for 25-30 minutes. When cool, sprinkle with powdered sugar. Cut into bars.

APPLE BUTTER BARS

Follow the above recipes but substitute 1 1/2 c. apple butter for the apple slices.

*

APPLE DUMPLINGS

2 c. brown sugar
2 c. water
1/2 t. cinnamon
1/2 c. butter
2 c. flour
2 t. baking powder

1 t. salt
2/3 c. shortening
1/2 c. milk
6 medium apples, peeled and cored
Sugar, Cinnamon, Nutmeg
Butter

Bring brown sugar, water, 1/2 t. cinnamon and 1/2 c. butter to a boil. Remove from heat. Sift flour, baking powder and salt. Cut in shortening. Stir in milk and roll dough out 1/4-inch thick on lightly floured surface. Cut into 6-inch squares. Put an apple on each square and sprinkle with sugar, cinnamon and nutmeg. Dot with butter. Moisten edges of squares and fold corners to center, pinching edges together. Place on ungreased baking dish. Pour syrup over dumplings and bake at 375 degrees for 35 minutes. Serve with cream. *(A lot of work, but they sure taste good on a cold, dull January day.)*

*

APPLE PUFFS

1 c. water
1 c. sugar
1/2 t. vanilla
1 1/2 c. flour
2 t. baking powder
1/4 t. salt

1/2 c. butter
3/4 c. milk
2 T. soft butter
2 T. sugar
1 t. cinnamon
5 apples, peeled and cored

Simmer sugar and water 5 minutes. Remove from heat and add vanilla. Sift flour, baking powder and salt. Cut in 1/2 c. butter. Stir in milk for a soft dough. In a separate bowl, combine sugar, 2 T. butter and cinnamon. Slice apples into a greased 8-inch baking dish. Pour syrup over apples. Drop dough by spoonfuls over apples making about 8 mounds. With a spoon, make a depression in each puff. Put some spice mixture in each. Bake at 425 degrees for 30-35 minutes until puffs are golden brown. Serve with cream.

*

PUFFY APPLE PANCAKE

3 eggs, separated   1/4 t. baking powder
3 T. sugar   2 T. butter
1/2 c. milk   1 c. diced apple
1/4 c. flour   1 t. cinnamon
1/2 t. salt   2 T. sugar

Beat egg whites until foamy. Gradually add sugar and beat until stiff. Beat egg yolks, milk, flour, salt and baking powder. Stir in apple and fold in egg whites. Melt butter in oven-proof frying pan. Spoon mixture into hot pan. Sprinkle on cinnamon and sugar. Bake at 450 degrees for 5 minutes. Reduce heat to 375 degrees for 10 minutes. Serves 2. *(Serve with Apple Cinnamon Syrup or Apple Walnut Syrup.)*

*

APPLE WALNUT SYRUP

3 T. butter   1/2 t. cinnamon
1/4 c. chopped walnuts   Dash salt
2 c. apples, sliced & peeled 1 c. maple syrup

Melt butter. Add nuts to brown slightly. Remove nuts and add remaining ingredients. Cover and simmer about 10 minutes. Remove cover and simmer 3 more minutes. Remove from heat and add nuts. Serve on waffles, ice cream, pancakes, custard, etc.

*

APPLE CINNAMON SYRUP

2 T. cornstarch   2 T. lemon juice
3/4 c. cold water   3 1/2 c. peeled and sliced apples
1 1/2 c. sugar   1/2 t. cinnamon

Mix cornstarch and water in saucepan until smooth. Stir in remaining ingredients and bring to a boil, stirring constantly. Cook until thick. Use like Apple Walnut Syrup.

APPLE COBBLER

1/2 c. butter	2 t. baking powder
1 c. flour	1/2 t. cinnamon
1/4 t. salt	1/2 c. milk
1 c. sugar	4 apples

Melt butter in 8-inch square baking dish. Mix dry ingredients together. Add milk and beat until smooth. Peel, core and slice apples. Pour batter into baking dish. Top with apple slices. Bake at 350 degrees for 45 minutes.

*

APPLE BROWN BETTY

1/3 c. sugar	2 c. fine dry crumbs
1/2 t. cinnamon	4 apples, pared and diced
1/4 t. salt	3 T. melted butter

Mix sugar, cinnamon and salt. Put layer of crumbs in greased baking dish. Cover with layer of apples. Sprinkle with sugar mixture. Continue until all ingredients are used, having crumbs on top. Pour butter on top. Cover dish. Bake at 375 degrees 40 minutes. Uncover last 10 minutes.

*

APPLE CRISP

8 medium apples	3/4 c. flour
1/2 c. water	1 c. brown sugar
1 t. cinnamon	1/2 c. butter
1/2 t. nutmeg	

Peel, core and slice apples thin. Place in greased casserole dish. Cover with water, cinnamon and nutmeg. Blend other ingredients until crumbly. Sprinkle over apples and bake at 350 degrees for 40-50 minutes.

*

CANDIED APPLE HALVES

6 apples (Jonathon)	1 c. water
1 c. sugar	1/2 c. cinnamon candies

Halve and core apples. Place cut side up in glass baking pan and pour sugar over them. Add water. Fill centers of apples with candies. Bake 350 degrees until candies have melted. Turn apples and continue baking until apples are transparent, about 1 hour.

*

RED CANDIED APPLES ON A STICK

12 small apples	1 c. water
12 wooden sticks	Four drops oil of cloves
3 c. sugar	12 cinnamon candies
3/4 c. corn syrup	

Insert stick in bottom of each apple. Heat sugar, corn syrup and water in saucepan, stirring until sugar melts. Add oil of cloves and candies. Cook, without stirring, until mixture form a hard piece that cracks when dropped in cold water--290 degrees on candy thermometer. Set pan over boiling water. Dip each apple into syrup. Let dry on buttered plate.

*

CARAMEL APPLES

1 lb. caramels	6 medium apples
2 T. water	6 wooden sticks

Melt caramels with water in double boiler. Insert stick in bottom of each apple. When caramels are melted and smooth, dip each apple into mixture, turning until well coated. (If desired, roll in chopped nuts.) Let dry on buttered plate or waxed paper. *(Guaranteed to cause cavitites.)*

*

APPLE LEATHER I

3 c. applesauce   1/2 t. cinnamon
1/2 c. sugar   1/4 t. nutmeg

Mix ingredients. Spread 1/4-inch thick in baking dish. Bake at 225 degrees about 3 hours. Cool and roll like a jelly roll. Cut into pieces and dust with powdered sugar.

*

APPLESAUCE CANDY

2 c. applesauce   2 envelopes unflavored gelatin
1 1/2 c. sugar   1/2 c. cold water
1/2 t. cinnamon   Powdered sugar
1/4 t. cloves

Heat applesauce, sugar and spices, stirring until sugar dissolves. Soak gelatin in water 5 minutes. Add gelatin to apple mixture, stirring well. Pour 1-inch thick into 8-inch square buttered pan. Chill until firm. Cut into squares and roll in powdered sugar.

*

HONEY BAKED APPLES

Apples   Honey
Raisins   Cinnamon

Core apples. Fill each with raisins. Pour honey in center to top of apple.
Sprinkle with cinnamon. Pour 1/-2 inch water in baking dish and bake apples at 375
degrees for 50-60 minutes.

*

SUGAR COATED BAKED APPLES

6 apples   2 T. melted butter
Sugar   1/2 c. flour
1/2 c. sugar   1 t. cinnamon
1 egg   1/4 t. salt

Peel and core apples. Roll in sugar and put in baking dish. Fill centers with
1/2 c. sugar. Beat together remaining ingredients. Drop 1 T. batter into each apple.
Bake at 375 degrees for 50-60 minutes.

*

PERFECT BAKED APPLES

6 apples   Cinnamon
Brown sugar   Butter

Core apples and pare a 2-inch strip along top. Place in baking dish. Fill
centers with brown sugar, a sprinkling of cinnamon and 1/2 t. butter. Pour 1 c.
water around apples and bake at 375 degrees for 50-60 minutes.

*

APPLESAUCE FRUIT CAKE

3 c. sweetened applesauce	1 t. nutmeg
1 c shortening	1/4 t. cinnamon
1/2 c. sugar	1 lb. mixed candied fruits
4 1/2 c. flour	1 lb. raisins
4 t. baking soda	1/4 lb. nuts

Heat applesauce, shortening and sugar, stirring until sugar dissolves. Cool. Mix in remaining ingredients. Bake at 300 degrees about 2-2 1/2 hours in greased loaf pans.

*

DRIED APPLE CAKE

1/2 c. dried apple slices	1/2 c. buttermilk
1/2 c. cider	1 t. baking soda
1/2 c. butter	2 c. flour
1 c. sugar	1/2 t. salt
2 eggs	1/2 t. cinnamon

Simmer apples and cider for 10 minutes. Beat sugar and butter. Add eggs. Mix buttermilk and soda together. Sift flour, salt and cinnamon. Add flour and buttermilk alternately to creamed mixture. Stir in apples. Bake in greased 9x13 inch pan at 350 degrees for 30-35 minutes. Frost with dried apple icing.

*

DRIED APPLE ICING

1/2 c. dried apple slices	3 1/2 c. powdered sugar
1/2 c. cider	1/4 c. melted butter

Simmer apples and cider for 10 minutes. Mix sugar and butter. Add apple mixture and beat until creamy.

*

CUSTARD APPLE CAKE

2 c. flour	1 c. water
1/2 c. oatmeal	1 c. sugar
1 c. brown sugar	3 t. cornstarch
3/4 c. butter	1 t. vanilla
1/4 t. nutmeg	2 apples

Mix flour, oatmeal, sugar, butter and nutmeg together. Save 1 cup. Pat rest of mixture on bottom of baking dish. Combine water, sugar and cornstarch in saucepan over medium heat until thick. Add vanilla. Slice apples into mixture. Pour into baking dish and sprinkle on crumbly mixture. Bake at 350 degrees for 50-60 minutes.

*

APPLE BUTTER CAKE

2 1/2 c. flour	1 c. sugar
1 1/2 t. baking soda	4 eggs
1 t. cinnamon	3/4 c. buttermilk
1/2 t. nutmeg	1 1/2 c. apple butter
1/4 t. salt	Powdered sugar
1/2 c. butter	

Sift flour, baking soda, spices and salt. Beat butter and sugar until fluffy. Add eggs. Beat in flour mixture alternately with buttermilk. Stir in apple butter. Pour into greased 9x13-inch baking pan. Bake at 350 degrees for 50 minutes. Cool thoroughly. Sprinkle with powdered sugar.

*

HONEY APPLESAUCE CAKE

1/2 c. shortening	1 t. nutmeg
1 c. honey	1/4 t. cloves
3 c. flour	1 1/2 c. applesauce
1 1/2 t. baking soda	1/2 c. raisins
1/2 t. salt	1/2 c. chopped walnuts
1 t. cinnamon	Powdered sugar

Cream shortening and honey. Sift flour, soda, salt and spices. Beat into creamed mixture alternately with applesauce. Stir in raisins and nuts. Pour into a greased 9x13-inch pan and bake at 350 degrees for 40-50 minutes. Cool and cut into squares. Sprinkle with powdered sugar.

*

AUSTRIAN APPLE TORTE

1 1/3 c. sifted flour	1 T. lemon juice
1/4 c. sugar	2 T. flour
1 t. grated lemon rind	2 T. sugar
1/2 t. salt	1/2 t. cinnamon
1/2 c. butter	3 medium apples
1 egg yolk	3/4 c. apple jelly

Stir 1 1/3 c. flour, 1/4 c. sugar, lemon rind, salt and butter in bowl until crumbly. Stir in egg yolk and lemon juice. Shape into ball. Press dough on bottom and 1 1/2 inches up sides of greased 9-inch springform pan. Scallop edges, pressing with thumb. Combine 2 T. flour, 2 T. sugar and cinnamon. Sprinkle half over dough. Peel, core and slice apples thinly onto dough. Sprinkle with flour mixture. Heat jelly and spread over apples. Bake at 375 degrees for 45-50 minutes. Cool. Loosen from pan.

*

1 c. sugar	1/2 c. cold coffee
1/2 c. butter	1 1/2 c. flour
1 egg	1/4 t. salt
1 t. baking soda	1 c. raisins
1 t. cinnamon	1/2 c. chopped nuts
1/4 t. nutmeg	2 c. chopped apples

Cream sugar and butter. Add egg. Beat coffee and dry ingredients alternately.
Stir in nuts, raisins and apples. Bake in 9x13-inch pan 45 minutes at 350 degrees.
Cut in squares and pour apple pudding sauce on top. *(See below.)*

*

APPLE PUDDING SAUCE

1/4 c. butter	1/4 t. nutmeg
1/2 c. sugar	1 t. vanilla
1 egg yolk	1 1/4 c. water
1 1/2 T. flour in saucepan	1 apple, diced

Cream butter and sugar. Beat in egg yolk, flour, nutmeg and vanilla. Gradually
add water. Cook until thick, stirring constantly. Mix in apples. Serve over cake.

*

CRUNCHY CARAMEL APPLE PIE

9-inch unbaked pie shell	1/2 t. cinnamon
30 caramels	Dash nutmeg
3 T. water	1/4 c. sugar
5 large apples	1/3 c. butter
3/4 c. flour	1/2 c. chopped walnuts

Melt caramels with water in saucepan over low heat, stirring occasionally until melted. Peel and core apples. Slice half the apples into pie shell. Pour half the caramel sauce over apples. Repeat with apples and sauce. Mix flour, spices and sugar in small bowl with butter until crumbly. Stir in nuts. Sprinkle over pie. Bake at 375 degrees for 45 minutes. *(About 80 jillion calories a slice, but who cares?)*

*

CRISPY APPLE CRANBERRY PIE

9-inch unbaked pie shell	1/2 t. nutmeg
5 large apples	1/2 t. cinnamon
1 c. canned whole cranberry	1/2 c. brown sugar
sauce	3/4 c. flour
1/2 c. brown sugar	1/4 c. butter
1 T. flour	

Peel and core apples. Slice into bowl and mix with cranberry sauce, 1/2 c. brown sugar, 1 T. flour, and spices. Pour into pie shell. Stir remaining ingredients together in small bowl until crumbly. Sprinkle over pie. Bake at 400 degrees for 35 minutes. Serve with ice cream.

*

APPLE CIDER PIE

2-crust, 9-inch unbaked
  pie shell
4 c. boiling apple cider
3 c. dried apple slices
3/4 c. brown sugar

2 T. flour
1/2 c. raisins
1/2 t. cinnamon
1 T. lemon juice
3 T. butter

Pour cider over apples and let stand 1 hour. Drain apples, reserving 1/2 c. liquid. Mix apples, sugar, flour, raisins and cinnamon and pour into pie shell. Pour lemon juice and reserved liquid over mixture. Dot with butter. Cover with top crust and bake at 400 degrees for 45 minutes.

*

APPLESAUCE CUSTARD PIE

9-inch unbaked pie shell
3 eggs
5 T. sugar

1/2 t. cinnamon
2 1/2 c. milk
1 c. applesauce

Beat eggs, sugar, cinnamon and milk. Mix in applesauce. Pour into shell. Bake at 450 degrees for 15 minutes. Reduce heat to 350 degrees for 30 minutes.

*

APPLE BUTTER PIE

1/2 c. apple butter
2 eggs
1/2 c. sugar

1 1/2 T. cornstarch
2 c. milk
9-inch unbaked pie shell and
  lattice top

Mix apple butter, eggs, sugar and cornstarch well. Beat in milk gradually. Pour into pie shell. Top with lattice strips. Bake at 350 degrees for 35 minutes.

*

PAPER BAG APPLE PIE

9-inch unbaked pie shell	1 t. cinnamon
5 large apples	1/2 t. nutmeg
1 c. sugar	1/2 c. flour
2 T. flour	1/2 c. brown sugar
2 t. lemon juice	3 T. butter

Peel and core apples. Slice into large bowl and toss with sugar, 2 T. flour, lemon juice and spices. Pour into pie shell. Mix remaining ingredients together in small bowl until crumbly. Sprinkle over apples. Place pie in large, brown paper bag. Fold open end over twice. Staple shut or seal with large paper clips. Bake at 400 degrees 50 minutes.

*

BRANDY & RAISIN APPLE PIE

2-crust, 9-inch unbaked pie shell	1 c. sugar
1/2 c. raisins	1 T. cornstarch
3 T. brandy	1 t. lemon juice
5 large apples	1 t. cinnamon
	1/4 t. nutmeg
	3 T. butter

Heat raisins and brandy in saucepan over low heat. Peel and core apples. Slice into bowl and toss with sugar, cornstarch, lemon juice and spices. Stir in raisins and brandy. Pour into pie shell and dot with butter. Put on top crust and slit for steam. Bake at 450 degrees for 45-50 minutes.

*

APPLE & CHEESE PIE

9-inch unbaked pie shell
5 large apples
2/3 c. sugar

2 T. flour
1 t. cinnamon
1/2 c. sour cream
1/4 lb. cheddar cheese, grated

Peel and core apples. Slice and arrange in pie shell. Mix sugar, flour, cinnamon and sour cream. Pour over apples. Sprinkle cheese on top. Bake at 400 degrees for 10 minutes. Reduce heat to 375 degrees and bake 40 minutes.

*

BROWN SUGAR APPLE PIE

2-crust, 9-inch unbaked
  pie shell
5 large apples
1 c. brown sugar
2 T. flour

1 1/2 t. cinnamon
1/4 t. nutmeg
Dash mace
1 T. grated lemon peel
2 T. butter

Peel and core apples. Slice thin and mix with sugar, flour, spices and lemon peel. Fill pie shell with apples. Dot with butter. Put on top crust and slit for steam. Bake at 400 degrees for 50 minutes.

*

APPLE & CREAM PIE

9-inch unbaked pie shell
5 large apples
1/2 c. sugar
1/2 c. water

1/2 t. cinnamon
Dash salt
1 egg
1/2 c. heavy cream

Peel and core apples. Cut into eighths. Bring to a boil in saucepan with sugar, water and spices. Cover and simmer 15 minutes. Drain, reserving syrup. Put apples in pie shell. Beat egg and cream together with syrup. Pour over apples. Bake at 350 degrees for 30 minutes.

*

DEEP DISH APPLE PIE

5 large apples	Dash salt
3 T. quick-cooking tapioca	1 t. cinnamon
3/4 c. sugar	1/2 t. nutmeg
1/4 c. brown sugar	Pastry for 8-inch dish

Peel, core and slice apples into thick pieces. Mix all ingredients together except pastry. Spoon into buttered deep 8-inch baking dish. Cover with pastry top. Cut in 6-7 slits. Bake at 425 degrees for 35-40 minutes.

*

APPLE CRUMB PIE

9-inch unbaked pie shell	1 t. cinnamon
5 large apples	1/2 t. nutmeg
1 c. sugar	1/3 c. butter
	3/4 c. flour

Peel, core and slice apples into pieces. Mix half the sugar with spices and sprinkle over apples. Put apples in pie shell. Mix remaining ingredients together until crumbly. Sprinkle over apples. Bake at 425 degrees for 10 minutes. Reduce oven to 350 degrees and bake 35-40 minutes.

*

RED CINNAMON APPLE PIE

2-crust, 9-inch unbaked pie shell	2 T. flour
	3 T. red cinnamon candies
5 large apples	1/4 t. salt
1 c. sugar	2 T. butter

Peel and core apples. Slice into bowl with sugar, flour, candies and salt. Mix well. Fill pie shell with mixture. Dot with butter. Put on top crust. Slit for steam. Bake at 400 degrees for 50 minutes.

*

PLAIN OLD APPLE PIE

5 large apples	1 t. cinnamon
3/4 c. sugar	1/8 t. salt
2 T. flour	2 T. butter
Dash nutmeg	2-crust, 9-inch unbaked pie shell

Peel and core apples. Slice thin and combine with sugar, flour, spices and salt. Fill pie shell with apple mixture and dot with butter. Put on top crust and slit for steam. Bake at 400 degrees for 50 minutes.

*

SOUR CREAM APPLE PIE

9-inch unbaked pie shell	1 egg
3/4 c. sugar	4 apples
1 t. vanilla	1/2 c. brown sugar
2 T. flour	1/3 c. flour
1 c. sour cream	1/4 c. butter

Beat together sugar, vanilla, flour, sour cream and egg. Dice the apples and add to mixture. Pour into pie shell and bake at 400 degrees for 25 minutes. Mix remaining ingredients until crumbly and sprinkle over pie. Bake for 20 more minutes.

*

DRIED APPLE PIE

2 c. dried apple slices	3/4 c. sugar
2 1/2 c. water	1/2 t. cinnamon
1 orange, rind & juice	2-crust, 9-inch unbaked pie shell

Soak apples overnight in water. Add orange rind and juice and boil until soft, about 30 minutes. Grind in food mill. Mix in sugar and cinnamon. Pour into pie shell and cover with top crust. Cut in slits. Bake at 425 degrees for 10 minutes. Reduce heat to 350 degrees and bake for 30 minutes.

*

INDEX

DESSERTS

Apple Brown Betty 32
Apple Cobbler 32
Apple Crisp 32
Apple Dumplings 30
Apple Puffs 30
Puffy Apple Pancake 31

JAMS, JELLIES

Apple Jelly 18
Apple Marmalade 18
Old Fashioned Apple Butter. . . .18

MAIN DISHES

Apple & Ham Casserole 25
Apple Meat Loaf 25
Apple Pork Balls & Sauerkraut . .26
Apple Stuffed Pork Chopes 23
Applesauce Meat Balls 25
Baked Apples & Sausage. 26
Meat & Apple Ring Patties 26
Sherried Chicken & Apples 24

PIES

Apple & Cheese Pie. 43
Apple & Cream Pie 43
Apple Butter Pie. 41
Apple Cider Pie 41
Apple Crumb Pie 44
Applesauce Custard Pie. 41
Brandy & Raisin Apple Pie 42
Brown Sugar Apple Pie 43
Crispy Apple Cranberry Pie. . . .40
Crunchy Caramel Apple Pie 40

Deep Dish Apple Pie 44
Dried Apple Pie 45
Paper Bag Apple Pie 42
Plain Old Apple Pie 45
Red Cinnamon Apple Pie. 44
Sour Cream Apple Pie. 45

PRESERVES

Apple Relish. 17
Crab Apple Preserves. 17
Spiced Crab Apples. 17

SALADS

Apple Slaw. 20
Golden Delicious Salad. 20
Red Apple Salad 20
Waldorf Salad 20

SNACKS

Apple & Cheese Snacks 7
Apple Butter & Cheese Waffles . . 6
Apple Pizza 6
Double Apple Sandwiches 7
Peanut Butter & Apple Sandwiches. 7

STUFFING

Apple Stuffing. 23
Apple Raisin Stuffing 22
Sausage Apple Stuffing. 23

SYRUPS

Apple Cinnamon Syrup 31
Apple Walnut Syrup. 31

VEGETABLES

Bavarian Apples & Cabbage 22
Scalloped Sweet Potatoes & Apples 22